# Bouldering

Level 8 – Purple

# Helpful Hints for Reading at Home

The graphemes (written letters) and phonemes (units of sound) used throughout this series are aligned with Letters and Sounds. This offers a consistent approach to learning, whether reading at home or in the classroom.

**HERE IS A LIST OF PHONEMES FOR THIS PHASE OF LEARNING. AN EXAMPLE OF THE PRONUNCIATION CAN BE FOUND IN BRACKETS.**

| Phase 5 | | | |
|---|---|---|---|
| ay (day) | ou (out) | ie (tie) | ea (eat) |
| oy (boy) | ir (girl) | ue (blue) | aw (saw) |
| wh (when) | ph (photo) | ew (new) | oe (toe) |
| au (Paul) | a_e (make) | e_e (these) | i_e (like) |
| o_e (home) | u_e (rule, cube) | | |

| Phase 5 Alternative Pronunciations of Graphemes | | | |
|---|---|---|---|
| a (hat, what) | e (bed, she) | i (fin, find) | o (hot, so, other) |
| u (but, unit) | c (cat, cent) | g (got, giant) | ow (cow, blow) |
| ie (tied, field) | ea (eat, bread) | er (farmer, herb) | ch (chin, school, chef) |
| y (yes, by, very) | ou (out, shoulder, could, you) | | |

**HERE ARE SOME WORDS WHICH YOUR CHILD MAY FIND TRICKY.**

| Phase 5 Tricky Words | | | |
|---|---|---|---|
| oh | their | people | Mr |
| Mrs | looked | called | asked |
| could | | | |

## TOP TIPS FOR HELPING YOUR CHILD TO READ:

• Allow children time to break down unfamiliar words into units of sound and then encourage children to string these sounds together to create the word.

• Encourage your child to point out any focus phonics when they are used.

• Read through the book more than once to grow confidence.

• Ask simple questions about the text to assess understanding.

• Encourage children to use illustrations as prompts.

This book focuses on /y/ and /ou/ and the alternative pronunciations of their graphemes. It is a Purple level 8 book band.

Can you work out which of these words have the same **ou** sound as **house**?

mouse

could

sprout

shout

mould

bounce

group

soup

Have you ever been bouldering? Bouldering is a sport that is all about finding the best way to clamber to the top of rock by choosing the best holds.

If you go bouldering at a gym, there will not be real rock. Bouldering gyms have lots of panels covered in different shaped holds.

Holds

A group of holds is called a problem. Before boulderers try to get to the top of a problem, they get a good look at it from the ground to scout out the best route to take.

Boulderers may have to try the same problem over and over to find the best way up.

In bouldering gyms, problems are set by people called routesetters. They drill different kinds of holds onto the panels. A big, round hold is called a sloper.

A thin hold is called a crimp. Boulderers need strong fingers to grip onto little holds like crimps. A crimp only has space for the very tips of the fingers.

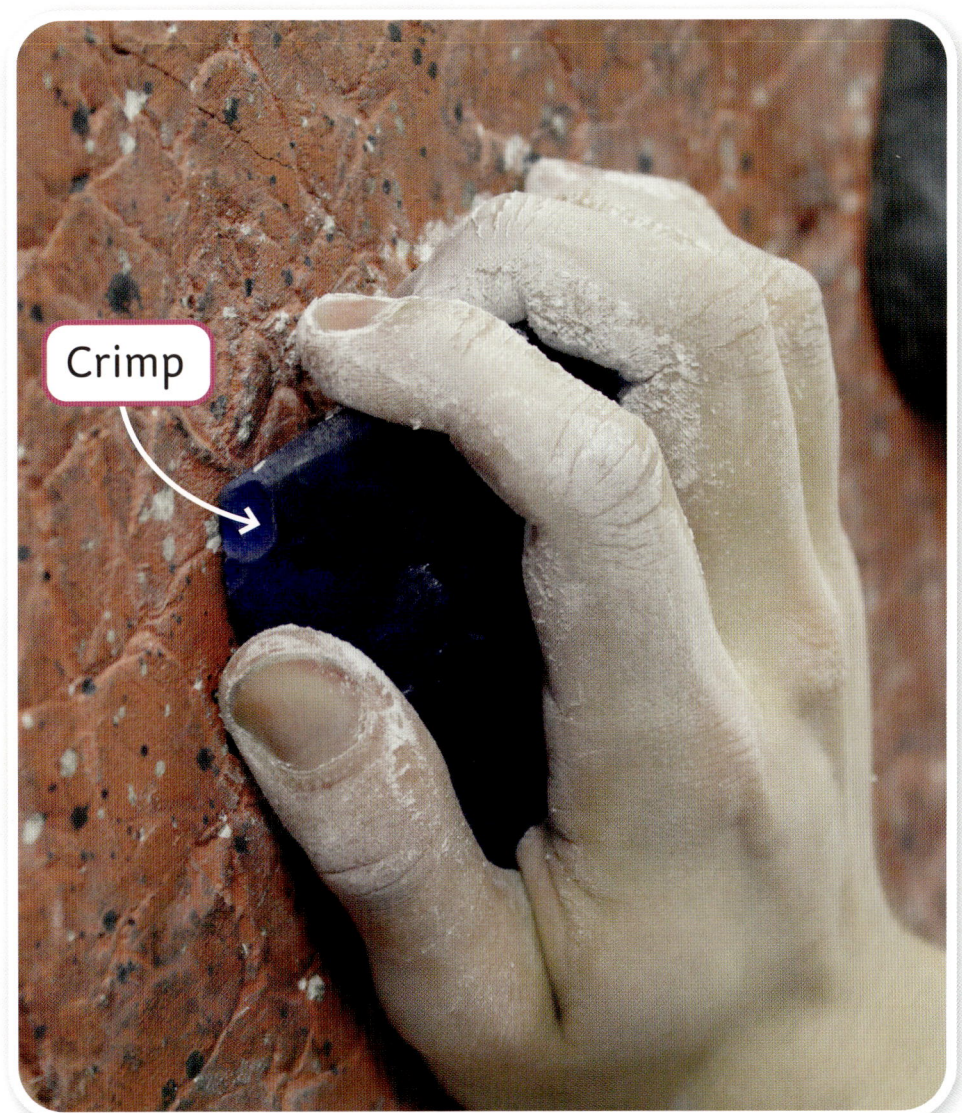

Crimp

Without the right gear, it would be easy to slip. Boulderers carry a pouch of powder with them to keep their fingers dry.

Powder

Boulderers use tight, rubber footwear, too. The rubber makes them sticky and gives the boulderer a good grip, even on tiny footholds. They can also hook their heels onto holds and trust that they will not slip.

Bouldering routes are normally pretty close to the ground, so boulderers do not have to worry too much about getting hurt if they do slip. There are soft mats under the problems, too.

Even with soft mats, boulderers could still get hurt if they landed badly. Boulderers may have people called spotters around them to help them drop safely onto the mats.

Spotter

Bouldering is most fun when you go as a group. Gyms have easy problems for new boulderers and hard problems for expert boulderers.

If you go on a bouldering trip outside, make sure that you bring safety mats. Some routes may not be safe even with mats, so never try to boulder without an expert there to help.

Safety mat

©2023 **BookLife Publishing Ltd.**
King's Lynn, Norfolk, PE30 4LS, UK

ISBN 978-1-80505-093-3

All rights reserved. Printed in China.
A catalogue record for this book is available
from the British Library.

**Bouldering**
Written by Charis Mather
Designed by Isabella Croker

# An Introduction to BookLife Readers...

Our Readers have been specifically created in line with the London Institute of Education's approach to book banding and are phonetically decodable and ordered to support each phase of the Letters and Sounds document.

Each book has been created to provide the best possible reading and learning experience. Our aim is to share our love of books with children, providing both emerging readers and prolific page-turners with beautiful books that are guaranteed to provoke interest and learning, regardless of ability.

**BOOK BAND GRADED** using the Institute of Education's approach to levelling.

**PHONETICALLY DECODABLE** supporting each phase of Letters and Sounds.

**EXERCISES AND QUESTIONS** to offer reinforcement and to ascertain comprehension.

**CLEAR DESIGN** to inspire and provoke engagement, providing the reader with clear visual representations of each non-fiction topic.

### AUTHOR INSIGHT:
### CHARIS MATHER

Charis Mather is a children's author at BookLife Publishing who has a love for reading and writing. Her studies in linguistics and experiences working with young readers have given her a knack for writing material that suits a range of ages and skill levels. Charis is passionate about producing books that emphasise the fun in reading and is convinced that no matter how much you already know, there is always something new to learn.

This book focuses on /y/ and /ou/ and the alternative pronunciations of their graphemes. It is a Purple level 8 book band.

**Image Credits** Images are courtesy of Shutterstock.com. With thanks to Getty Images, Thinkstock Photo and iStockphoto.
Cover – Maria Ticce, sajinnamu, Sharomka. p4–5 – zhukovvvlad, nuclear_lily. p6–7 – Duet PandG, Jacob Lund. p8–9 – frantic00, Brian Maag. p10–11 – UfaBizPhoto, Zakirov Aleksey. p12–13 – michelangeloop, UfaBizPhoto. p14–15 – asife, Andrew Angelov.